Mary Douglas Glasspool

Alleluia!

May God bless you in your new ministry! Bill M Lemore +
and Lori M. Lowe +

April 23, 2010

A Gift
of Laughter
from
The Reverend
William McLemore
in tribute to

Rainbow Village, Inc.

Published by
The Brack Group (GA) Inc.
dba GwinnettForum
in conjunction with
United Writers Press, Inc.
P.O. Box 326
Tucker, Georgia 30085-0326
www.unitedwriterspress.com
1-866-857-4678

ISBN: 1-934216-10-0
ISBN-13: 978-1-934216-10-1

Printed in the USA.

A Symbol of Promise

Throughout history, the rainbow has been a symbol of promise and God's covenant of mercy for humankind.

"When the bow is in the clouds,
I will look upon and remember the
everlasting covenant between
God and every living creature…"
Genesis 9:16

Rainbow Village has a covenant of mercy
for people who need our help today.

Each night, more than 20,000 people
find themselves homeless in Atlanta.

Sixty percent of them are
mothers and children.

With your help, Rainbow Village
can provide some of these families
the assistance required to
overcome the hurdle of homelessness
and return to a
stable and productive life.

Table of Contents

Foreword   vii

Preface   ix

The Beneficiaries, Objectives, & Solutions   xi

The Board of Directors   xv

The Cartoons

Out of the Mouths...   1

Love Thy Neighbor...   27

For the Love of It   51

All About Me   67

Environmental Effects   93

The Miracle of Technology?   109

The Church in General   127

In Their Own Words   153

   Board Members   155

   Excerpts from Letters Written to Rainbow Village   157

   Excerpts from Letters from Former Families   161

Outcome Statements   172

Contact Information   174

FOREWORD

At first glance, one might wonder why we chose to showcase Rainbow Village with cartoons.

The answer is simple really. Rainbow Village is, in a word, about healing. And to borrow the old cliché, laughter *is* the best medicine.

As a former psychotherapist, I watched as those patients of mine who managed to retain a sense of humor seemed to heal faster from the blows life dealt them. As a human, I've experienced the grace of God through those who refused to let me wallow in my own self-pity, dragging me out to a funny movie or a party with friends.

We know that Jesus wept...but I'll bet He laughed much more often. And I would argue that He guides Bill McLemore's pen when he sits down to draw his signature cartoons just as surely as He speaks through him when he stands in the pulpit.

It is no accident that tears and laughter bring the same physical and emotional relief. I have both laughed and cried until I found myself on my knees. I know which one of the two I prefer to get me there. On my knees, I mean.

So...as you give to aid Rainbow Village in fulfilling its mission to help smooth the road for those who've encountered rough spots on their journeys, accept this little book as a gift of healing in return.

It comes not *from* us, but *through* us.

Vally M. Sharpe, M.A.
CEO, United Writers Press, Inc.

PREFACE

This is a preface to a book about Rainbow Village which is in the process of being written. Usually the author of a preface has the book or a manuscript to look at when doing it. Since that is not possible for me here, I instead will write a "Preface to Rainbow Village."

It began with a gift from a member of Christ Church, Episcopal, Norcross, Georgia, who had previously moved away to New Jersey because of business. In spite of the distance, he maintained his bond to Christ Church. When he heard of the plans for a "homeless" ministry and of the old house on Norcross-Tucker Road leased from the Georgia Power Company that we got on a $1.00/year lease, he asked, "How can I help?"

The house was a shambles with a broken roof and flooded basement—uninhabitable completely. He gave me a check for $25,000!

We planned, planned, and planned—changing our minds as we went over the various ways to establish a homeless ministry. The dominant models for us in the community were all doing a good job, we thought, but they were sort of...well...paternalistic. We had a sense of unease about that pattern and after much debate, settled on a different approach. And that is the story.

I wrote an article for the parish newsletter, "The Communique," in July 1990 about our ideas for the ministry (not yet named). The article was titled "A New Deal," and in part, it said:

We are going to use our old house to give someone a NEW DEAL. We are still forming our ideas about this and invite you all to join in. We think a new deal should include Initiative. The ones who are helped need to be partners in the enterprise. They will need to be allowed to and *expected* to take the initiative. A new deal should include Development. Our partners should start from some place and move to some place. They need to know where they are and where they want to go. And the new deal should include Achievement. They will need to feel like they have really done something, and were not just done unto. Charity is not helpful, but Initiative, Development, and Achievement are.

These have been our guiding principles since 1990 when we made two apartments in the old house. Rainbow Village (at first Rainbow House) is now a much bigger ministry, embracing the loving efforts of many people from many churches, companies and community groups in a vibrant, lifegiving outreach to families in need.

The key ideas described back in 1990 actually work! I have seen it over and again. Nancy Yancey will tell someone applying for admission to the program, "You must have a job and a car to get into Rainbow Village," when they have neither one. When they show up three or four days later, with both job and car, they are on their way into a world of Initiative, Development, and Achievement.

The Reverend Joel P. Hudson
Chairman Emeritus–Rainbow Village Board

Rainbow Village, Inc.

The Beneficiaries

Families with Children
who have become homeless due to domestic violence,
family break-up, unemployment, medical problems, and
perpetuating cycles of abuse and/or poverty

Volunteers and Staff

Objectives

Financial Stability
Family Stability and Strength
Job Stability
Emotional Stability
Spiritual Strength

Solutions

Shelter, Food, Community
Life Skills Training
Counseling
After School Program
Children's Programs

What is the mission of Rainbow Village?

- The mission of Rainbow Village is to provide families in domestic or economic crisis a healing environment in which to rebuild their lives through a community-based transitional housing program. Rainbow Village currently serves families with children in north metro Atlanta.

How did Rainbow Village start?

- Rainbow Village began as the "Rainbow House" ministry of Christ Episcopal Church in 1991 and grew into a separate non-profit corporation (1995). It now operates with an annual budget of over $500,000. Since its inception, Rainbow Village has served over 150 families—12 families at a time.

Where is Rainbow Village located?

- In the cities of Norcross, Georgia (four single family homes) and Duluth, Georgia (an eight-unit apartment complex).

What are the responsibilities of Rainbow Village families?

- Families must commit to self-sufficiency plans and reach those goals within one year.
- Adults must be employed and have workable transportation.
- In lieu of rent, families are required to open and maintain savings accounts, pay a portion of utilities, and a program fee. Monthly financial reports/budgets are monitored by Rainbow Village staff.
- All school-age children must participate in the Rainbow Village After School Programs and summer camp at the Fowler YMCA.

Why do Rainbow Village families succeed?

- Involvement with Rainbow Village is based on initiative and accountability.
- Families live, not in isolation, but in a caring, supportive community.
- A dedicated staff and community offers much needed support during the transition period, including assistance with realistic goal-setting and attainment.
- Assistance with development of financial management skills enables families to save in order to acquire homes of their own, reduce debt, improve credit ratings, and maintain savings.
- The after-school program helps children excel academically and socially.
- "Graduates" are required to continue participation in Rainbow Village programs and to mentor others.

How is Rainbow Village funded?

- Individuals like YOU!
- Churches
- Corporations
- Foundations
- The state of Georgia and Gwinnett County

How else can you make a difference?

- Assist with the children's programs
- Provide meals for evening classes
- Offer assistance with maintenance of homes and grounds
- Give in-kind donations of home furnishings, autos, supplies, etc.

When God told Abraham, who was a hundred at the time, that at the age of ninety his wife Sarah was finally going to have a baby, Abraham came close to knocking himself out—"fell on his face and laughed," as Genesis puts it (17:17). In another version of the story (18:8 ff.), Sarah is hiding behind the door eavesdropping, and here it's Sarah herself who nearly splits a gut—although when God asks her about it afterward, she denies it. "No, but you did laugh," God says, thus having the last word as well as the first. God doesn't seem to hold their outbursts against them, however. On the contrary, he tells them the baby's going to be a boy and that he wants them to name him Isaac. Isaac in Hebrew means *laughter*.

Why did the two old crocks laugh? They laughed because they knew only a fool would believe that a woman with one foot in the grave was soon going to have her other foot in the maternity ward. They laughed because God expected them to believe it anyway. They laughed because God seemed to believe it. They laughed because they half-believed it themselves. They laughed because laughing felt better than crying. They laughed because if by some crazy chance it just happened to come true, they would really have something to laugh about, and in the meanwhile it helped keep them going.

Faith is "the assurance of things hoped for, the conviction of things not seen," says the Epistle to the Hebrews (11:1). Faith is laughter at the promise of a child called Laughter.

—from *Wishful Thinking: A Seeker's ABC*
HarperSanFrancisco
© *1973, 1993 Frederick Buechner*

Out of the Mouths...

The children of Rainbow Village are challenged to grow to their full potential. Due to the instability of the family, many children are behind both socially and academically. The After-School Program extends the learning that takes place in school and provides a variety of activities based on the interests of children in the program.

14

20

23

Love thy Neighbor...

We all need to be loved and accepted as we are, to know that others will be there to share our pain and joy. But how often do we stay in the secure places in our lives when we should step out of the boat? There is nothing quite like the experience of giving of oneself—it is only then that we realize that we have given the gift to ourselves. Give of your time—you won't regret it.

"For you were called to freedom, brethren; only do not use your freedom as an opportunity for the flesh, but through love, be servants of one another. For the whole law is fulfilled in one word, 'You shall love your neighbor as yourself.' But if you bite and devour one another take heed that you are not consumed by one another."
—Galatians 4:14,15

I LOVE THE LOOK ON THEIR FACES WHEN GUYS WITH MORE THAN ONE WIFE COME UP HERE AND FIRST SEE ALL OF THEM!

50

For the Love of It

The annual budget of Rainbow Village, Inc., a 501(c3) organization, is now over $500,000.

We are funded by churches, corporations, foundations, the state of Georgia and Gwinnett county, and incredible individuals like you.

To make a tax-deductible donation, please visit
www.rainbowvillage.org

or send a check or money order to
Rainbow Village, Inc.
400 Holcomb Bridge Rd.
Norcross, Ga. 30071
Phone: (770) 446-3800

61

All About Me

In the beginning of this little book, we listed the beneficiaries of Rainbow Village. You may have noticed that volunteers and staff are among them.

That's because though we often get caught up in concentration on the almighty "I," volunteers who give their time to Rainbow Village discover that it is not only the lives of the families serviced that are changed.

There but for the grace of God go we all.

83

91

Environmental Effects

Homelessness is a devastating experience for families. It disrupts virtually every aspect of family life, damaging the physical and emotional health of family members and interfering with children's education and development.

Nationally, 58 percent of homeless persons are women and children. The average age of a homeless person is nine years old.

Rainbow Village provides supportive services including case management, life skills training, domestic violence support groups, and family and children's counseling in conjunction with Consumer Credit Counseling, the Gwinnett Extension Service, Kaiser Permanente, the Partnership Against Domestic Violence, and the Fowler YMCA.

95

"THE LAST PLAGUE!"

The *Miracle* of Technology?

Whatever happened to "high tech, high touch"? You know, that idea that with technology we'd be able to do the same amount in less time, freeing us up to spend time with each other again?

It's still possible...

Visit our website at

www.rainbowvillage.org

and you'll see.

111

118

HTTP://WWW.GOD.COM

The Church
in General...

*"The love of Christ strengthens us to be the church to
each other and the world. Many of us have acknowledged
how much this love we share sustains us in our lives
together. We share in the hope of the kingdom of God
embracing us to love one another, in spite of our
differences, in times of trouble and times of peace. To
'drink of the pure, spiritual milk that enables us to grow
into salvation and taste the goodness of the Lord.'*

*The families of Rainbow Village are a part of a
community that shares the goodness of God in their lives.
Those seeking a home and shelter from the storms of life
come to Rainbow Village through the doors of Christ
Church to be embraced by the body of Christ. We are to
open our doors to those in need."*

*—adapted from a sermon of The Reverend Nancy Yancey
Executive Director of Rainbow Village*

138

FORMER DRILL SERGEANT BECOMES ACOLYTE WARDEN

RITE II   RITE I

146

150

In Their Own Words

Board Members

Through my years at Rainbow Village, I learned several very important things. These lessons have become an integral part of who I am. *One thing I have learned is that the people that we serve at* Rainbow Village *are truly our neighbors.* In many if not most ways, they are just like me. They are members of my community, and they are wonderful people who often just need a little help, as I certainly do from time to time. *Another thing I have learned is that individuals can make a big difference.* There are plenty of people who come to Rainbow Village to do things as simple as serving a meal or raking some leaves. These people add immeasurably to the character and the success of Rainbow Village. *A third thing I have learned is that miracles are happening here and now.* Rainbow Village truly changes the lives of many people, both those who serve and those who are served. You don't have to be around a place like Rainbow Village very long to truly understand what a miracle is!

Finally, and most important for me, I have learned that I am truly blessed. I have met many residents of Rainbow Village, who at first glance seem to have many problems, yet tell me with such joy how blessed *they* are. Through them, I have realized that we are *all* truly blessed, and all too often we take our blessings for granted. *I have also come to realize that* Rainbow Village *is continually blessed by God and by the people who so selflessly give of their time and resources.* This past year started out on shaky footing, but ended up as one of the best years ever for Rainbow Village. Because of the donations of some generous individuals and foundations, the generosity of those that participated in our golf tournament and our fabulous auction, the diligent work of the staff and many volunteers, and because of the blessing of a wonderful grant from HUD, I can truly say that Rainbow Village is finally beginning to have a solid financial future. For the first time ever, I am beginning to realize that not only will Rainbow Village continue to operate, but that we will potentially have the resources we need to grow and fulfill the dream to make Rainbow Village an even richer place than it already is.

Thanks be to God and to all of those that have contributed to the prosperity of Rainbow Village!

Howard Jetmundsen
Chairman of the Board
2004-2006

155

There are many wonderful organizations in our society that direct their efforts toward helping people and Rainbow Village is one of them—one with a special calling. Christ taught us to love one another. But how does one go about that? We all go about living our lives trying to help others on an individual basis or collectively by combining our efforts with others to handle greater challenges. Much of the time we are inconsistent and are not thinking of helping others until an opportunity presents itself. And yet, on the other hand, we would like to do something to feed the hungry of the world but because of the magnitude of the problem we shake our heads and hope that it will be taken care of by the large relief agencies. So where can we make a difference?

One way that I like to think about helping others has been best put by Charles Dickens in *A Christmas Carol* when he says "Mankind is our business." This brings it home for me, as business is a daily event that we are all engaged in, whether it is the business of running a business, household, or other enterprise. It is ongoing. And when you can help people better themselves and learn how to be a productive part of society, holding their own and understanding that helping others is an integral part of their lives, you have just described what Rainbow Village is all about. You are doing more than feeding someone for a day; you are equipping them for a lifetime. You are making a difference! I know that the Rainbow Village programs work because we have graduates of Rainbow Village eager to help and others engaged in helping those in the program make their way.

I spent over thirty-six years in healthcare supporting people—making a difference in people's lives both mentally and physically—and mankind was my business. Today Rainbow Village allows me to support others by making a difference in people's lives. Graduates of Rainbow Village learn what it means not only to receive a hand up but to give a hand up to others. It multiplies!

In Rainbow Village's case, you help families and each member of the family, from children forming good habits and feelings about themselves to adults doing the same. I can't think of a better organization to support and to ask others to support than Rainbow Village—an organization making a difference!

Franklin M. Rinker
Chairman of the Board
Rainbow Village, Inc.

Excerpts from Letters Written to Rainbow Village

"Will you help us?"

"I am the mother of a 30 year old drug–addicted daughter. I have five beautiful granddaughters, a set of twin girls, age 12, and a six, eight and ten year old who are depending on me to care for them or they will be sent to foster care. I am 57 years old, working a minimum wage job. I can't do this alone. Will you help us?"

"My wife has bone cancer. I have a good job as a welder but the medical expenses above and beyond what my insurance will cover are more than I can handle. My wife, my three year old daughter and I cannot make it much longer on our own. Will you help us?"

"My husband beats me up every day. He has told me there is no way I could possibly make it in the world and raise our three children without him. I have been sleeping in the car while my children sleep inside with him. Even though he beats me up, he does not beat my children. But they hear and see him abusing me. I now have a job and am working every day after dropping off my children at school and returning home to get ready for work after he leaves. I need a home; I need a place of safety for me and my children. Will you help us?"

"I have been living on the street since the age of fourteen when my parents through me out," said a 30-year-old mother of two children, ages 8 and 10. "I am a drug addict. I am sleeping in my storage room with what little possessions we have. My children are staying with friends. I want to live a better life. I don't know how. I don't know where to go or what to do. Will you help us?"

"I have been a prisoner in my home for almost two years. My children go to school and lead fairly normal lives, but my husband will not allow me to go out of our house. A neighbor finally realized something was strange, knocked on my door one day and asked me if I needed help. She told me about Rainbow Village. My two boys and I need help. Will you help us?"

"I am forty-two years old. I am a drug addict and an alcoholic. I have two wonderful sons that deserve a mother that can provide them a home and a future. I want things to be different for us. Will you help me and my children?"

Excerpts from Letters from Former Rainbow Village Families

"I am so thankful that I have had the privilege to be a part of Rainbow Village and be transformed into the mother and person that I am called and destined to be..."

When I first came to Rainbow Village I was broken, scared, and had very low self worth. I made a very important step, though, when I made the decision to call Rainbow Village. For the first time in my life I did not get anyone else to help me. I found the number for Rainbow Village and called. I had decided that enough was enough! I was tired of going around the same mountain and was ready for a change, not only for me but for my children. I knew that God had made a way for me to be a part of Rainbow Village for a reason. Like most tenants, I went through the usual stages. First I was angry that I had to follow so many rules. I was distant and did not talk, and then one day I blossomed. I had been going to my weekly meetings with my life coach, Mary Jane LaBonte, and also attending my monthly meetings with our counselor, Stacy Collins, and I was set free from the cocoon of just settling and transformed into a self sufficient person.

Like everyone else, I have had my ups and downs, but I feel that without the love, support, and lifting up that I received at Rainbow Village, I would be circling that same ole mountain of self doubt and insecurity.

I lost a son nine years ago, and I had never grieved his death. I had suppressed all of the grief and pain and went on like the hard-headed woman that I had become. But through the love and understanding that I received from the Rainbow Village staff, I was able to mourn my son's death and was able to release him. I learned that I was not in control. This resulted in my giving my four children who are alive the freedom to become the young men and women that they are called to be. One day my 13-year-old son, Joshua, and I were in the car and we were listening to Kelly Clarkson's song, "Because of You," and the song says, "Because of you I never strayed too far from the sidewalk," and my son said to me, "Because of you I never even got to *see* the sidewalk." Even though he was joking in his own way, it was true. I had been so over-protective of my children I had deprived them from being children. I had home-schooled my children and never really let them experience having friends and socializing. I was set free and was able to send my children to school and guess what? They did fine! They have all come out of their shells and it is amazing what just letting go and letting God in will do in your life as a family.

I am so thankful that I have had the privilege to be a part of Rainbow Village and be transformed into the mother and person that I am called and destined to be. If anyone out there is blessed enough to be a resident at Rainbow Village, please don't waste your time. Take that time to listen, learn, and to make changes and choices that are needed to transform your life.

Now I get the privilege to mentor the new residents that come in. I feel so blessed to be free enough to be able to tell my story and help others with their transformation. I love everyone at Rainbow Village and know that I will be in their family for life.

My name is Amy and Rainbow Village gave me a new life. I can still recall it in my mind as if it was yesterday…I remember 8 years ago going before the panel to describe why my family should be selected for the last unit available in Rainbow Village. I was living with my ex-husband in a very nice home in Peachtree Corners. We had divorced 2 months prior. Knowing that I had no other place to go, he used that to his advantage and agreed to have us to remain living in the same home. Staying there, I was subject to all sorts of abuse. In June of 1996, after he had forced himself upon me, I knew I had to leave.

I had no idea where I would go or no place to turn but to God. I started praying and asking God to show me the way. I called the Gwinnett County Helpline and told them about my situation. They told me about Rainbow Village and I was given a contact number. I had never heard of transitional housing before and did not know what I was getting into. I got an application and filled it out, and was given an appointment time to go before the board.

On June 18, 1996, there I stood in front of the panel with tears streaming down my face filled with pain, rejection, and fear, holding my baby boy in my arms; I answered all the questions the panel had to ask.

Not knowing If I would be accepted or not, I went back home and start packing. He got angry, asking me where did I plan to go? Had I landed another guy who would take me in with a baby? Not even caring that the baby was his own son, his own flesh and blood. Within two long weeks, I was told that my family was chosen. I was very happy but nevertheless I felt bad for the families that were not chosen, and I promised myself I would be out within 6 months to give someone else a chance. We were given a very small cozy cottage home to live in—complete with everything including a phone.

At Rainbow Village, I met new friends; I met people who truly loved me and did not want anything back in return. I was taught how to budget, save, and to take care of my household of all boys, who were ages 15, 9, and 10 months at the time. In January of 1997 I moved into my own townhouse after 5 1/2 months of living at RV.

Rainbow Village had set me up to win. I have a little savings and I landed a great job with an advertising company. I left RV feeling secure and in control...

Once in my townhome, my ex found out where I was living, and I was intimidated by him to the point that I started dating and sleeping with him again, and it was the worst thing that could have happened.

This time he became even more physically abusive to me and I had him sent to jail. Rainbow Village and Nancy Yancey stuck by me, helped me to obtain an attorney, and set me up for counseling so I could get away from being co-dependent, which I felt I had become. My ex continued for years stalking me and trying to control me. But I wasn't about to fall into that trap once again.

I got myself back on track within 3 months and started to focus on me and my family...

Within a year I rented a house and joined a church of which I have been a member for 7 years. My oldest son graduated from high school in 1999 and from there he went on to Mercer University and graduated from there in 2003, obtaining 3 majors in Biology, Chemistry and Spanish. He is currently utilizing them all working at a company near our home. At graduation he was asked what was he going to do (putting on hold his life long dream of becoming a doctor). He said, "Move back home, work, and help my mom to raise my brothers...she needs all the help she can get."

It's 2004 and we are all doing quite well. I am an office manager for a company in Atlanta going on 5 years now.. My middle child is a junior in high school and plays football and basketball, and runs track…He's a typical teenager…My youngest is almost 9 years old and he is into reading, soccer and a straight A student… The only thing that saddens me is the fact that his father refuses to see him because I will not allow him to control my life.

With the faith I have, and with God on my side, we will continue to do well. When life gives you lemons, add some sugar, shake it up and make lemonade, and enjoy it because life is so short. I will forever be grateful to Rainbow Village. And to Nancy Yancey!!

I love you guys!

Advice for those who may be in the shoes I was in. When you are given an opportunity to start over, make the best of it… Put God and your children first. You can live without a man, but living without God or my three boys would have been impossible. I have no regrets about my life. I am happy I had the guts to leave. Rainbow Village was there to support me…and they stuck by my side until I had wings to fly on my own. We need more Rainbow Villages because there are a lot of women with children who are in the shoes I once wore…

God is good…and I am grateful.

When I first came to Rainbow Village, I did not know what to expect. I was very exited but scared at the same time. I knew before entering the program it was going to change my life and I was ready for a change.

I am a single mom and I have 2 wonderful children that are 8 and 9 years old. When my children heard that we were going to a program with other families and children, they were so happy and full of joy. The first few days that we entered the program the children adjusted very well and loved everything about the program. They enjoyed going to the dinners there on Tuesday nights because they love to eat but they truly enjoy it because they can be themselves and play and have fun with all the children and volunteers. Everyone that has been a part of Rainbow Village has been so wonderful and we appreciate their hard work—just loving us for who we are and accepting us just the way we are. The meetings on Wednesday nights offer family counseling for the children. It has been amazing to watch my children express their feelings, thoughts, and emotions together. We were able to laugh, cry, and share our true feelings and discuss everything together as a family.

My children and I learned how to love each other with all our hearts and understand each other better. I learned how to love myself and my children in way that I never did before. I also learned to accept myself and to accept the way God made me.

Living at Rainbow Village has been a wonderful experience and very challenging. It was not easy at all but the support, encouragement and loving families here at Rainbow Village made it easier for us. We are very grateful to have the opportunity to be at Rainbow Village.

You want a one-page essay describing what Rainbow Village has meant to me, and what role it has played in my life? I am not sure where to begin. How do you describe being giving the gift of life?

I have been involved with Rainbow Village for 10 years—as a resident, a volunteer & mentor, a board member and as staff.

Through the years and the many different titles, I have been blessed with the gifts of strength, love, patience, and family through Rainbow Village. I came into this organization alone, scared and beaten down. I was pregnant with my third child and had two small children under two. I was leaving an abusive marriage and coming from another state.

I came into Rainbow Village so distrusting of people and feeling like I had to make it on my own; Rainbow Village showed me that I did not have to live that way anymore. I have learned what family truly means. I learned how to reach out, get help, turn around, and help those behind me.

I have learned how to manage my money through the life skill lessons I was given. I successfully purchased a home. I learned how to trust others. I have been blessed to have the tools now to be able raise happy and well adjusted children, and to know that we are never alone and will always have the support of Rainbow Village. It does take a village to raise a child.

Most important, Rainbow Village never once looked upon me as anything other than a woman trying to put her life back together. They understood I was looking for a helping hand up, homeless yes, helpless no!

Sometimes it takes a village to make a house a home.
By Jennifer Stalcup Staff, Correspondent.
Reprinted from *Gwinnett Daily Post* March 29, 2003.

When Mildred Alderman was evicted from her apartment last fall, she was faced with the reality of being homeless.

Through determination and help from Mattie Goss, a counselor at Atlanta Technical College, she found Rainbow Village, a non-profit transitional housing program that offers homeless families and their children safe homes and a strong support system.

"I wound up living in my car for a couple of days, and I was so sad," said Mildred, a single mother of a 13-year old son still under her care and a grown daughter.

In between classes at ATC, where she graduated in May as a Practical Nurse, Mildred says she usually spent her time in the hall laughing and talking, but after being homeless for a few days she was depressed and needed some solitude.

As Mildred stood outside contemplating her future, Goss noticed her state and asked what was wrong. Mildred told her the whole story, which included the cold, non-responsive stares she got from her previous apartment manager when she pleaded for guidance.

"I told her that darn nursing program ain't so easy either," Mildred said with a grin. "But here I am — I stayed in school, and I'm making A's and B's."

Not believing a stranger could offer such kindness but willing to try anything at this point, Mildred ventured to Goss' office that day, and they began a computer search of possibilities. The Salvation Army was chosen and Mildred went there with her son that evening.

"My son looked at me like, 'What are you doing?' I just felt like dying looking at his face," Mildred said of the experience. "I looked around and saw lots of people on drugs and just started crying and left. I suffer from clinical depression, and going though all that made me just want to crawl under a rock. The next day I almost didn't go to school, but I'm sure glad I did."

170

Goss had an alternative plan to share with Mildred, which she shared after class the next day. She told Mildred about a place that sounded top notch—Rainbow Village.

Rainbow Village facilities are located in Duluth, Snellville, and Norcross, and each family must meet certain criteria to be accepted into the program. In order to qualify, one must have a job, own a reliable car, have children to care for, and to be in a state of homelessness. No drug use is tolerated and random inspections of the homes are carried out.

Each family is allowed to stay in a completely furnished home, which includes a computer, for six months to a year, with extension and graduation benefits to those who aren't quite ready to strike out on their own.

Participants reap an array of benefits that go beyond shelter.

Outcome Statements

*Rainbow is committed to the following
organizational outcomes:*

Families will be made strong
- *Children's grades will improve while they are residents at Rainbow Village*
- *Families remain intact with children/partners remaining with the family.*
- *Debt is reduced by time of moving to permanent housing.*

Women will be free to leave domestic violence situations.
- *90% of women do not go back to batterers during their term with us.*

Families will obtain permanent housing.
- *80% of families will obtain rental housing.*
- *20% will purchase their own homes.*

Parents will obtain better paying jobs.
- *95% of families obtain a better paying job during their stay with Rainbow Village*

The cycles of homelessness, domestic violence, and poverty will be broken.

What Now?

You can make a difference.

Rainbow Village, Inc.

To make a tax-deductible donation,
please visit
www.rainbowvillage.org

or send a check or money order to
Rainbow Village, Inc.
400 Holcomb Bridge Road
Norcross, Ga. 30071
Phone: (770) 446-3800